INTRODUCING DINOSAURS

OVIRAPTOR

BY SUSAN H. GRAY · ILLUSTRATED BY ROBERT SQUIER

The Child's World

Published in the United States of America by The Child's World®
1980 Lookout Drive • Mankato, MN 56003-1705
800-599-READ • www.childsworld.com

ACKNOWLEDGMENTS
The Child's World®: Mary Berendes, Publishing Director
The Design Lab: Kathleen Petelinsek, Art Direction and Design;
Victoria Stanley and Anna Petelinsek, Page Production
Editorial Directions: E. Russell Primm, Editor; Lucia Raatma, Copy Editor;
Dina Rubin, Proofreader; Tim Griffin, Indexer

PHOTO CREDITS
©Dmytryp/Dreamstime.com: cover, 2–3; ©Hulton-Deutsch Collection/
Corbis: 10–11; American Museum of Natural History: 11 (bottom), 16–17,
18–19, 19 (right); ©Bettmann/Corbis: 12; ©Custom Medical Stock Photo:
16 (left)

LIBRARY OF CONGRESS CATALOGING-IN-PUBLICATION DATA
Gray, Susan Heinrichs.
 Oviraptor / by Susan H. Gray; illustrated by Robert Squier.
    p. cm.—(Introducing dinosaurs)
 Includes bibliographical references and index.
 ISBN 978-1-60253-240-3 (lib. bound: alk. paper)
 1. Oviraptor—Juvenile literature. I. Squier, Robert, ill. II. Title.
 QE862.S3G69552 2009
 567.912—dc22   2009001627

TABLE OF CONTENTS

WHAT WAS OVIRAPTOR?

Oviraptor (OH-vuh-rap-tur) was a small dinosaur. It lived millions of years ago. Its name means "egg **thief**."

Oviraptor was not very large. Most other dinosaurs were much bigger.

WHAT DID *OVIRAPTOR* LOOK LIKE?

Oviraptor weighed about the same as a third-grader. It had a long neck and a long tail. *Oviraptor* had **slender** legs and ran quickly. Its arms were short but strong. Each hand had three long fingers.

Oviraptor's small size helped it to be a swift runner. This speed came in handy when bigger dinosaurs were chasing it.

Oviraptor had a sharp beak like a parrot. It also had a tall, hornlike bump on the top of its head. The bump was flat on the sides. **Scientists** call the bump a **crest**.

Oviraptor's hard beak helped it to catch its meals. Its sharp claws were also useful in getting food.

10

WHY WAS *OVIRAPTOR* CALLED AN "EGG THIEF"?

Scientists discovered *Oviraptor* about eighty-five years ago. They found **fossils** of its skeleton. The skeleton was with some dinosaur eggs. Scientists thought it had been stealing the eggs before it died. They said it must have been an egg thief. So they named it *Oviraptor*. Later, they realized they were wrong. *Oviraptor* was actually protecting its own eggs. Poor dinosaur! It is stuck with the wrong name!

A group of scientists headed into the desert in the 1920s hoping to find new fossils (far left). They discovered Oviraptor on this trip. The trip was led by Roy Chapman Andrews (near left).

11

WHAT WAS LIFE LIKE FOR OVIRAPTOR?

Oviraptor slept, ate, and took care of its babies. It built a nest and laid eggs. Its eggs were long and shaped like hot dog buns. *Oviraptor* kept them warm and safe. One by one, the eggs hatched. *Oviraptor* fed its babies and watched over them.

Roy Chapman Andrews (above), became the director of New York's American Museum of Natural History. He wrote a number of books about his adventures. The first Oviraptor fossils found came from a nest (right).

13

Most dinosaurs ate either plants or meat. But not *Oviraptor*—it ate just about anything! *Oviraptor* ate leaves, fruits, eggs, and insects. With its speedy legs, it chased small **prey**. It cracked clamshells with its beak. Then it ate the meat inside.

Oviraptor sometimes chased smaller animals when it got hungry. Other times, it just ate plants.

HOW DO WE KNOW ABOUT *OVIRAPTOR?*

Oviraptor left fossils of its bones and eggs. The fossils tell us about *Oviraptor*'s life. For instance, its bones were **hollow** and very light. A dinosaur with light bones could run quickly.

Scientists must work slowly and carefully so they do not break the fossils they are digging up (right). Oviraptor's hollow bones (above) are even easier to break than other fossils.

17

Fossils do not tell us everything, though. They do not explain why *Oviraptor* had a crest. They do not tell us what their babies ate. So people keep looking for more fossils. Someday, we will know more about this little dinosaur.

Scientists continue to search for new Oviraptor *fossils. In 1993, scientists discovered a fossil of an* Oviraptor *skeleton on top of its eggs (above).*

WHERE HAVE OVIRAPTOR BONES BEEN FOUND?

Mongolia

NORTH AMERICA

EUROPE

ASIA

Atlantic Ocean

Pacific Ocean

AFRICA

SOUTH AMERICA

Indian Ocean

AUSTRALIA

Map Key

Where *Oviraptor* bones have been found

Southern Ocean

WHO FINDS THE BONES?

Fossil hunters find dinosaur bones. Some fossil hunters are scientists. Others are people who hunt fossils for fun. They go to areas where dinosaurs once lived. They find bones in rocky places, in mountainsides, and in deserts.

When fossil hunters discover dinosaur bones, they get busy. They use picks to chip rocks away from the fossils. They use small brushes to sweep off any dirt. They take pictures of the fossils. They also write notes about where the fossils were found. They want to remember everything!

Fossil hunters use many tools to dig up fossils. It is very important to use the right tools so the fossils do not get damaged.

GLOSSARY

crest (*KREST*) A crest is a ridge, tuft, or other tall growth on an animal's head.

fossils (*FOSS-ullz*) Fossils are preserved parts of plants and animals that died long ago.

hollow (*HOL-loh*) If something is hollow, it has an empty space inside.

Oviraptor (*OH-vuh-rap-tur*) *Oviraptor* was a small dinosaur that lived millions of years ago.

prey (*PRAY*) An animal that is caught and eaten by another animal is called prey.

scientists (*SY-un-tists*) Scientists are people who study how things work through observations and experiments.

slender (*SLEN-dur*) Slender things are things that are thin.

thief (*THEEF*) A thief is a person or animal that steals things.

BOOKS

Goldish, Meish. *The Oviraptor Adventure: Mark Norell and the Egg Thief.* New York: Bearport Publishing, 2006.

Gray, Susan. *Oviraptor.* Mankato, MN: The Child's World, 2004.

Mattern, Joanne. *Oviraptor.* Pleasantville, NY: Gareth Stevens Publishing, 2009.

Parker, Steve. *Dinosaurus: The Complete Guide to Dinosaurs.* New York: Firefly Books, 2003.

WEB SITES

Visit our Web site for lots of links about *Oviraptor*:

CHILDSWORLD.COM/LINKS

Note to Parents, Teachers, and Librarians: We routinely verify our Web links to make sure they are safe, active sites—so encourage your readers to check them out!

INDEX

ABOUT THE AUTHOR

Susan Gray has written more than ninety books for children. She especially likes to write about animals. Susan lives in Cabot, Arkansas, with her husband, Michael, and many pets.

ABOUT THE ILLUSTRATOR

Robert Squier has been drawing dinosaurs ever since he could hold a crayon. Today, instead of using crayons, he uses pencils, paint, and the computer. Robert lives in New Hampshire with his wife, Jessica, and a house full of dinosaur toys. *Stegosaurus* is his favorite dinosaur.